BARLOW EXPLORES THE U.S.A.

BY JESSICA CROMWELL
ILLUSTRATED BY ROD JOHNSON

© 2010 by Jessica Cromwell. All rights reserved.

No part of this book may be reproduced, stored in a retrieval system, or transmitted by any means without the written permission of the author.

ISBN 1-4507-2050-2

Barlow the Boxer™

Visit www.barlowtheboxer.com to learn more fascinating facts and enjoy a virtual travel experience with Barlow!

Off we go to places unknown.

...let's discover America!

We're off on an adventure to explore the U.S.A. We'll stop in awesome places and have fun along the way!

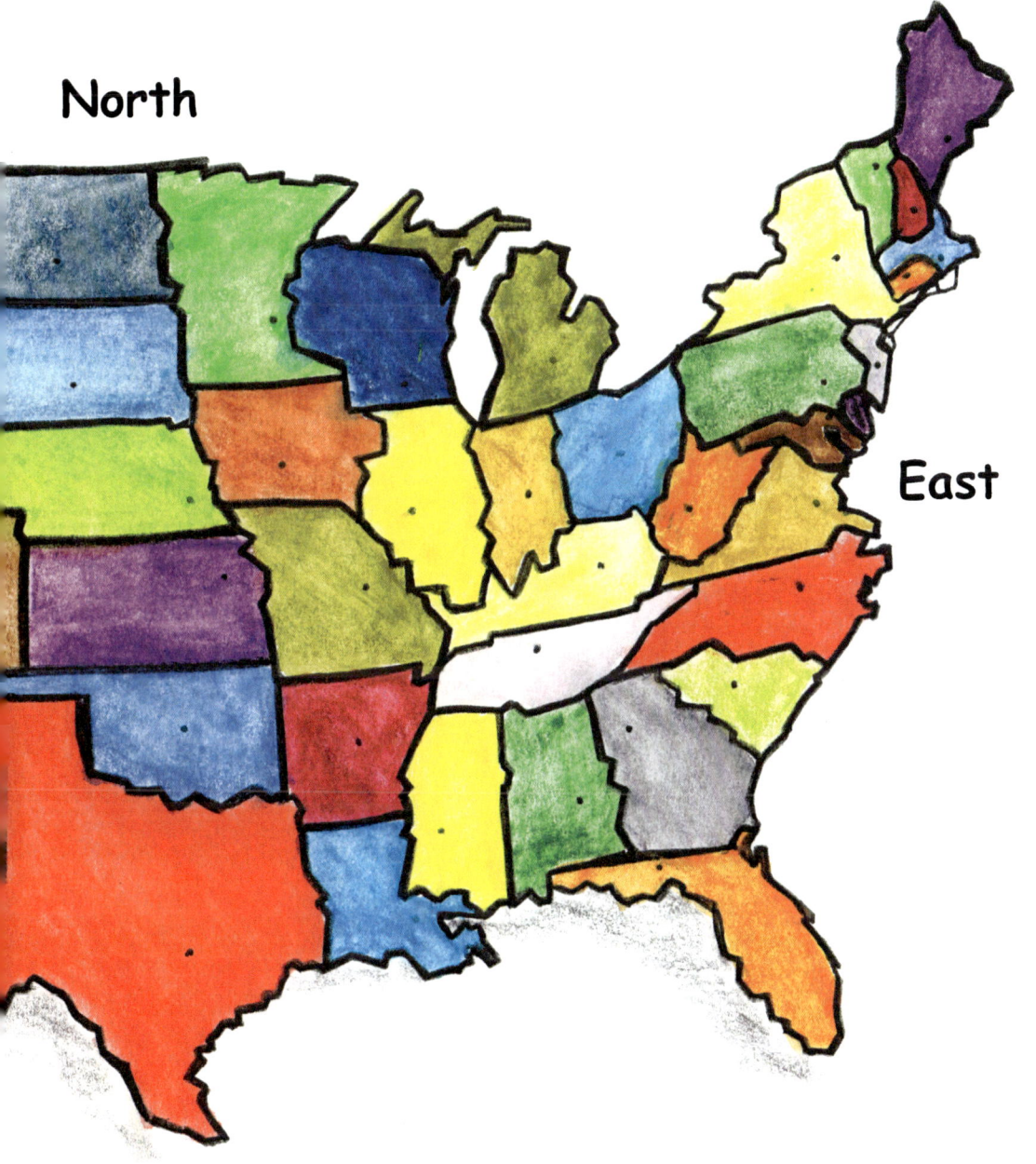

The United States of America has many special traits. It's time for us to visit landmarks around our 50 states!

Before we start our journey, though, there's something you should know.

Our nation is on the planet earth, which is quite large and grand. Let's talk first about our borders, so you know what's around our land.

Canada

The Gulf of Mexico and Mexico border our southern coast. Canada is to the north of us. Both are friends of ours, we boast.

The Atlantic Ocean is to our east and the Pacific is to our west. The coastlines make for beautiful scenery, as you may have guessed.

Two states are extra special as they are not connected to the rest. They're on the Pacific Ocean side, far into the west.

Atlantic Ocean

Gulf of Mexico

Mexico

From the cold air of Alaska, let's move south to the islands of Hawaii. Two thousand miles from the mainland, beauty is in large supply.

Now let's get back to the mainland, the west coast is where we'll begin. There is a spot in northwest California that is sure to make us grin.

The Redwood Forest is where we'll find the world's tallest trees. If we hike on one of the many trails, we'll feel as tiny as can be!

Yellowstone National Park is where it can be found. We will see bison, bear, moose and other wildlife all around!

Off to the Grand Canyon, south now we go. In northwest Arizona we see the Colorado River flow.

It took millions of years for the river to carve the canyon walls so steep. At some points along the way it's 6,000 feet deep!

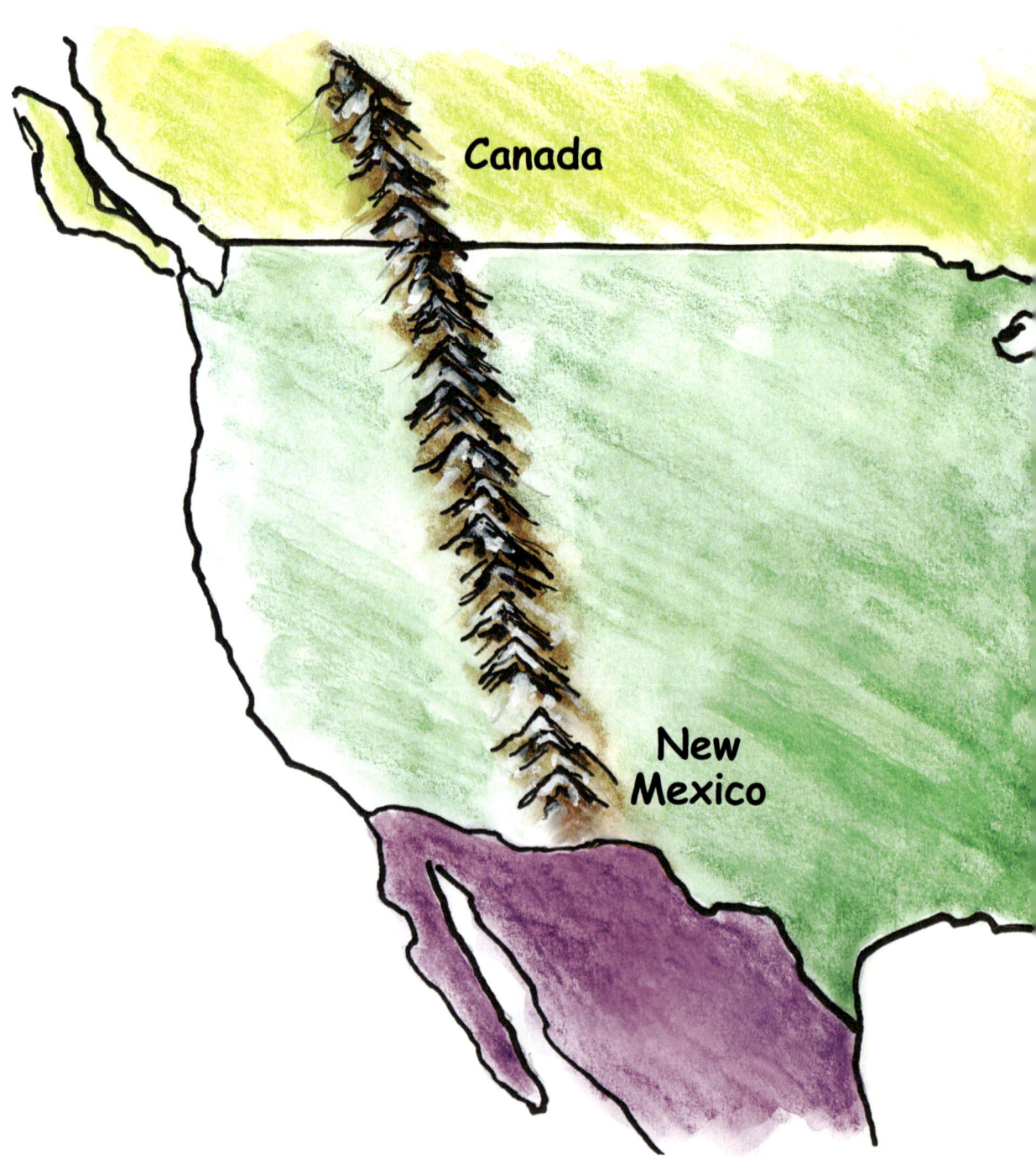

On we go to Colorado and the Rocky Mountains' highest peak. It stands so very tall, at over 14,000 feet.

The range spans from Canada down to New Mexico and is full of diverse beauty that gives us quite a show.

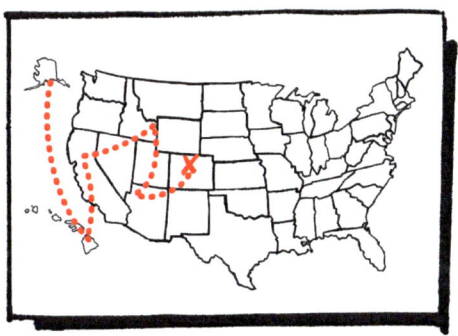

Down we head to the Lone Star State. Texas is home to oil fields, farming and many things great!

It was once a large part of Mexico, but joined America after the Battle of the Alamo.

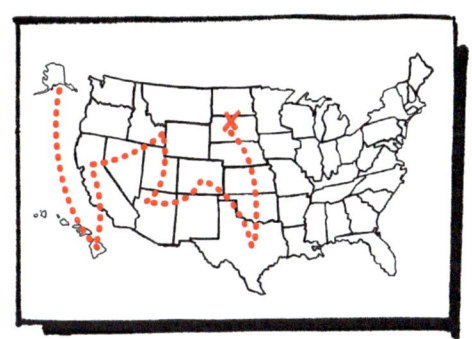

Straight up to South Dakota,
there's a place we can't ignore.
Faces of Presidents Washington,
Jefferson, Lincoln and Roosevelt
are found at Mount Rushmore.

Carved out of the mountainside
and completed in 1941,
this spectacular sculpture
cannot be outdone!

There's something special about our next stop as we will see our country's bird. During winter in Illinois, thousands of bald eagles can be seen and heard.

There are forests and swamp lands and the 10,000 islands to explore. We'll see osprey and manatee and wildlife galore!

Jefferson Memorial

We'll visit monuments and museums,
the list of important places is long.
We must try to see them all
before we can move on!

Lincoln Memorial

We go north now just a jump, skip and a hop...through Maryland and Pennsylvania, on to our next stop.

Between New York and Canada, there is a place so grand. Niagra Falls has more water flowing over it than any in the land!

Although it's hard to say good-bye, our journey must now end. We've seen and done so many things, I'm proud to call you my friend!

Good-bye my friends.
I hope you enjoyed our journey!
Don't forget to visit
www.barlowtheboxer.com
to learn more fascinating facts
about landmarks around the U.S.A.

Your friend,
Barlow the Boxer